THE NEW TRAIL

by

Otto Scheuzger

translated by Joyce Baldwin

OMF BOOKS LONDON

First printed in Germany 1961

First printed in Great Britain 1963

Reprinted 1964, 1966
New edition . . . . September 1976

ISBN 0 85363 114 X

Made in Great Britain
Published by Overseas Missionary Fellowship
Newington Green, London N16 9QD
and printed by Stanley L. Hunt (Printers) Ltd.
Midland Road, Rushden, Northants

Contents

1. The Long Night

The dark silhouettes of squatting men could only just be seen in the smoky glow of the wood fire. They were all pressing close to its warmth; or perhaps they were seeking the protection of the mighty fire-spirit. The shack was filled with smoke, darkness and the stench of decay.

'Boom, boom, boom!' went the steady rhythm of a drum. Lateng was thumping vigorously on the tightly-stretched calf-skin. It sounded dull and uncanny, like an approaching storm.

About six yards from the fire, near grandmother's sleeping quarters, young Paure was jumping about. Playing a bamboo flute he leapt high in the air, turned and ducked, sat back on his heels and then braced his skinny body ready for another leap. He seemed tireless, and his instrument never stopped for a moment.

The men by the fire chattered unconcernedly, even though the drum went on booming and rumbling. They knew it had to go on, to drive away the evil spirits.

The women and girls, slim and barefooted, were squatting beside a body that lay motionless on a rough board. Their shrieks and wails swelled like a stormy wind and then subsided to a gentle sobbing, only to rise up again and become more and more sinister and turbulent. Dirty hands gently stroked the waxen face of the recumbent form.

'Mbla, beautiful Mbla! Why have you left us so soon?' moaned Ka in a tear-choked voice, and the lament rose again from the others.

Above the corpse hung the demon altar. Strips of paper dangled from the altar shelf; blood and the flesh of sacrifices lay upon it. Incense sticks were burning all round. The men crouched by the fire and passed the bamboo pipe from one to the other. They were all smoking hookahs and keeping up a lively conversation.

Tusang moved unsteadily from one neighbour to the

next, filling up the only cup again and again with rice wine. If only it was all over and his wife's corpse buried! He felt as if he couldn't bear to stay there any longer—but where else was there to go? The noise of drum and flute and the moaning of the women filled the whole village. What about the jungle? No, certainly not there! The spirits would be sure to attack him. Perhaps Mbla's soul had already been turned into a man-eating tiger that would tear him to pieces in the forest. . . .

'Horrible, horrible,' he murmured, then stopped, terrified. 'No! I mustn't accuse the spirits. I must bear it all patiently.'

If only he could find an answer! He was only 18 years old and had already lost his wife. Why had it happened to him?

'She was a lovely girl,' he thought regretfully. 'She was strong, so she didn't find the work in the fields too hard. She was a good cook, and skilful at spinning, weaving and sewing. She would certainly have borne me a healthy child every year. . . . And yet, only four months after our wedding she fell ill. Shua Ying ordered two chickens to be sacrificed to the red spirit . . . but that didn't do any good. I had to sacrifice the last pig, and still the red spirit wasn't appeased. And now Mbla's lying there, dead, lifeless, rigid. . . . What good have all the offerings done? None! Old Kau, whose spirit can drink human blood, bewitched her!' Passionately Tusang clenched his fists.

'If only I could get my own back on Kau!'

But he could do nothing, absolutely nothing.

Even Re, the village chief, wouldn't dare to take action against Kau. He was afraid of the magician and tried to keep the peace with him. And the Thai authorities down in Tak weren't concerned with the interests of the mountain tribes in the backwoods.

'If only I were a Thai! Then I could have gone to school. I'd be living in a fine house, and I wouldn't just be a despised savage!'

Already the first glimmer of daylight was greeting the forest village, and Tusang shivered as he went back into the shack. There were still a few men squatting round the fire. He sat down beside them and mechanically stuck a log into the fire. The men were talking about their young chief.

'Lanang says that Re is going to buy from Wangchau and fetch her at the full moon.'

Tusang pricked up his ears, interested. 'Has Lanang agreed now?'

'Lanang can't object if his son wants to marry a second wife!'

'The old man wants Re to get an heir, anyway.'

'He's rich—he can afford to have several wives.'

'Re's been living with Mpheng for six years now, and she still hasn't borne him any children. She's like a dead tree with no fruit on it. Come what may, Re must buy a second wife.'

'But Mpheng is so proud—what will she say about that?' Tusang inquired.

'Well, she storms and weeps all day long and half the night. But that won't do her any good, if Re wants to have children!'

Tusang said nothing and stared into the flames.

The lament for the dead was still going on, and a smell of decay filled the dark hut. The flute kept up its shrill whine and wail. The drum boomed and thundered with muffled sound.

Tusang yawned, and sauntered over to the corner where he slept.

'What a good thing I've got some opium,' he thought. 'At least I can be sure of happy dreams in my sleep. I gave my silver for my wife; my pigs have been slaughtered—and now my wife is dead! So you, my dear opium pipe, are the only friend I have left!'

2. The Shelter in the Fields

The little group was working hard. A great deal of time had been wasted during Mbla's illness when Tusang and his mother had had to take turns nursing her. Then, when she died, there were the long days of lament. Everyone had to stay at home, even though the rice was ripe, and monkeys and birds were stripping the fields.

Grandmother Sheng and Tusang's sister were busily cutting handful after handful of golden rice. They tied the little bundles together with straw and threw them aside. Tusang and his brother Nshua finished making the little shelter of leaves, and went to help.

The sun was burning mercilessly down on the sea of forest and on the little fields where the hill-farmers were hard at work, sweat trickling down their faces. Tusang hardly said a word. His pale face with dark rings round dreamy eyes betrayed that the 18-year-old had become a slave to opium. His hands were trembling and his legs swayed. The sun was still not quite overhead when he unrolled his bamboo mat on the floor of the shack and lay down near the little lamp, hands grasping the opium pipe. He was soon lost in dreams of another world. His mother gave him a contemptuous look and mumbled something, but Tusang saw and heard nothing. The others went on cutting.

Vigorous blows were coming from the neighbouring rice-field where Shua Ying's family were threshing their rice.

'Another two or three days and Shua Ying will have finished,' mumbled Grandmother Sheng. 'Then he'll be able to go into his poppy fields—the seed boxes are ripe for slitting already. Why ever did Mbla have to die? She hadn't been able to help at all. One has to pay dearly for a daughter-in-law and then she dies in the very first year. What a frightful loss!' The old woman grumbled discontentedly to herself. 'And now Tusang's fallen into the grip of opium!'

There was nothing she could do about that. All Méo

men smoked opium, a few in moderation, but most of them to excess.

'Ka,' she shouted suddenly to Nshua's wife, 'haven't you cooked the rice yet? Come on, hurry up, we're all hungry!'

The young woman silently obeyed. Soon a little fire was burning under the battered sooty pan resting on three stones. Dinner consisted of rice, cabbage, and a little pork. The whole family ate out of the pan with their fingers, wiping their hands afterwards on a girdle or skirt.

After a short rest they went back to work again. The sun was already going down towards the sunset mountains and their limbs were aching.

'We'll have to reap hard for another two days,' said Grandmother Sheng, 'and then it will be high time we started on the opium. I hope the monkeys and birds won't eat our rice in the meantime!'

'Yes, so do I,' Nshua agreed, 'but we can't go on threshing any longer. We must begin to harvest the opium. Opium's much more important than rice.'

'I must go back to the village tomorrow,' the old woman told them. 'Wang is ill.'

Tusang looked at his mother in astonishment. 'Where have the spirits bitten?' he asked inquisitively.

'They nearly always bite Wang in the head. She smokes a lot of opium, but that doesn't cure her headache. She asked me yesterday to go and give her my magic potion.'

'Isn't Wang capable of exorcising the headache spirits herself? Surely she's an expert at things like that. She's had wide experience of egg-magic and egg-gazing especially.'

'Ha! Plenty of people understand egg-magic and egg-gazing, but that's no help against the headache spirit.'

Ka's little ones were already fast asleep beside her on the old bamboo mat. Just one blanket was sufficient for all three.

The night wind was playing with the leaves that hung down from the roof of the little shelter. In the distance a bamboo flute was wailing. As the sound came nearer it was possible to distinguish voices.

'Tusang, Tusang, are you there?'

'Yes—come in!'

Tsunshua appeared, with his two brothers. A bent old man followed, out of breath. Nshua pushed a wooden stool towards him.

'Sit on this, Shua Ying; the tree trunk is no place for a grandfather!' Tusang blew into the fire, while Grandmother Sheng offered the guest something to smoke. The flute fell silent. The youths crouched by the fire and played with the burning logs.

'Haven't you finished cutting the rice yet?' Shua Ying asked.

'In another two or three days it will be cut,' Nshua told him, 'and then we'll move on to the opium field.'

'I'm hoping for a good opium harvest.'

'So am I.'

'I hear that the Thai are going to seize a large part of the opium as tax,' Tsunshua put in.

'The Thai have wicked hearts,' said Nshua fiercely. 'All they want is money and opium.'

'Yes, they think they can treat us as slaves, because we don't have any books.'

'They don't really bother about us at all.'

'It's only when they want our opium that they come and bring their expensive cloth.'

'Yes, they forbid us to plant opium but they are glad we do; otherwise they wouldn't have anything to smoke.'

'And they make plenty of money out of trading with us!'

Grandmother Sheng got up, stretched, yawned, and lay down beside those who were already asleep. She loosened her belt and rolled herself up in her blanket.

Tusang and Shua Ying were lying on the bamboo mat by the fire. A vegetable-oil lamp was burning between them, and in their hands were their opium pipes.

'Wouldn't you like to marry again, Tusang?'

'Yes, I'd certainly like to, but I've neither silver nor opium. Who's going to give his daughter to a man who's got nothing?'

'You're young and healthy,' Shua Ying encouraged him.

'Not one of us knows as much Thai as you do. You'll be sure to get a good-looking wife.'

'If only I were a Thai! Knowing the Thai language is no use to a despised tribesman in the forest!' It sounded more bitter than he had intended. Shua Ying made no reply, but just went on sucking at the pipe. Tusang continued, 'And now I'm an opium sot into the bargain!'

'You mustn't talk like that, son.' The old man coughed and went on, 'While you are still young you can cut it down. Go out with the young men again when they go to find wives. You're sure to find one you can pair up with.'

'We're going to bed, Father,' Tsunshua said, getting up and poking his brothers awake.

When the neighbours had gone, Tusang carefully put his pipe into the little bamboo basket that stood in the corner. He unrolled his mat and waited for sleep to come. But his tired head was burning. Familiar scenes from the past kept coming before him. He saw his wife's face—where was she now? She'd been a good wife, and he couldn't believe she might have become a man-eating beast. But who was to know? Who did decide the fate of the dead, anyway?

Someone was snoring, and one of the children cried out in his dream. Tusang pulled his red blanket right up to his nose even though the night wasn't really cold. The fire had gone out. A few stars peeped through the holes in the roof. It was high time he got a little sleep before morning claimed the forest once more.

3. In the Chief's Shack

Tusang went into the Chief's shack and saw in the half-light a colourful group of people. Lanang looked up when he heard the door creak.

'Tusang, kau tua la!'

'Tua la!' he returned the greeting, and squatted beside the crackling fire. Young and old were jostling the Thai men in the middle of the shack.

'What are they selling?' Tusang asked.

'Come and look at this lovely cloth, Tusang,' called La enthusiastically.

The merchant had noticed Tusang now, and was calling something to him in Thai.

'So it's you, Lien,' replied Tusang, looking pleased. He got up quickly and pushed his way through the group to the centre pole of the shack. The others made way for him grudgingly. The merchant called Lien was about 18 years old. He was short, but his skin was darker than that of the Méo.

'How smart he looks in his shorts and shirt!' thought Tusang, looking admiringly at his friend. 'His clothes are much nicer than our long black trousers, held up with red girdles. And this tight black jacket is so hot in the day-time!'

'That red stuff there is especially suitable for girdles,' Lien told the women pressed around the baskets. 'It's only ten grams of opium a length.'

'Let me see, let me see!' they were all shouting at once. Right hands fingered the splendid, red cloth, while left hands clasped a little bit of opium, wrapped up in a banana leaf. They complained about the high price, and bargained backwards and forwards, but in the end all the women bought something.

'Haven't you anything else?' asked one man, who was getting bored.

'Indeed I have. Look at this black cloth—it comes from the foreigners' land and so it's very expensive.'

'Do the foreigners weave cloth then as well? I thought they only built flying machines.'

Lien laughed. 'The foreigners can do everything! We Thai buy all our goods from the foreigners. These shorts come from abroad, so does the shirt and my shoes, too. Foreigners also made this watch here.'

The Méo listened open-mouthed. 'It can't be true! The foreigners are not human beings like us. They are evil spirits!'

'That explains how they have the power to conjure up all these things.'

'Yes, that's it!' agreed everyone, and that settled the matter. Tusang was disappointed. He really wanted to know more.

'Lien, isn't there anything else you Thai can do besides plant rice fields? You've got all kinds of wonderful things, like schools, books, lovely houses. . . .'

Lien replied proudly. 'Of course, we Thai can do all kind of things, but what's most important is that we have the best rice there is on earth. It doesn't grow in the foreigners' land. The foreigners are dependent on us. They make all sorts of things which they sell to us, but in exchange we sell them our rice, because we always have plenty.'

The people had listened intently, but only a few understood what Lien was saying. Tusang translated the speech for them, enjoying the chance to show off his Thai. Everyone shrieked in horror and amazement, and people found it difficult to believe—was it possible that there could be a land where no rice grew? Were these people so stupid that they didn't even know how to plant rice? Or perhaps the soil wasn't good enough? Tusang didn't know the reason either.

'Even though the foreigners have their magic to produce flying machines, and trousers and cloth and watches, what use is it to them if they haven't any rice? What a good thing they can buy their rice in Thailand, or they would starve to death!'

This news was discussed in the village for a long time. People were thankful once more to be Méo, and not to have to live in a foreign land where there was no rice.

Tusang was standing in front of the Chief's shack trying to make up his mind what to do next. There didn't seem much point in going home—he had neither wife nor children, and now he hadn't even any more opium.

Suddenly a torch shone in his face and made him jump. 'Tusang, what are you doing here?' exclaimed his friend Nshu Seng.

'Nothing. Where are you going, Nshu Seng?'

'I want to try to exchange a pig for some cloth. My children need new clothes.'

The little man with the pock-marked face flung open the door again, and Tusang followed him into the shack.

'What about my pig?' Nshu Seng asked Lien. The merchant turned from his meal, and wiped his mouth on the back of his hand. 'I'll buy it if it's healthy.'

'Thoroughly healthy. I shouldn't sell it if I didn't need new clothes for my children. They had nothing new last year, and they're running about in rags.'

'Haven't you got any more opium?' asked Lien, chewing away at the fish.

'No, I've spent it all. There isn't even any left for my own pipe.'

'Well, I advise you to plant more opium in the autumn so you'll have enough next year. This time I'm prepared to accept your pig. I'll come and look at it in the morning. Of course, I can't give you as much cloth for it as for opium.' Lien turned back to his supper.

The fire was still flickering in Shua Ying's shack. The women had already been asleep for a long time, and the old man was squatting on the stool by the fire, surrounded by a few neighbours. His sons hadn't come in yet, even though the log, reaching almost to the door at sunset, had burnt away to a short stump.

'The dogs are barking furiously again,' commented Nshua.

'It's full moon, and they are seeing the spirits which we humans cannot,' the old priest told him.

'Animals are clever. Cats never stay in a house where there are many spirits, do they? That's why people say, "Where there are cats and dogs the people must be good".'

'And yet the spirits come to us all,' said another neighbour.

'Yes they come to us all, but people whose hearts are white will soon drive off the evil spirits with their sacrifice.'

'It must have been lovely when there were no spirits.'

Nshua laughed. 'There have always been spirits!'

'No,' said Shua Ying, 'long, long ago, when there were no Thai and no Chinese, we lived in a beautiful great land. We owned many rice fields and raised fat pigs; we kept splendid horses and had many chickens. No one was ill and no one afraid. Neither was opium known. At that time there were no spirits. But that is a long time ago.'

'Yet even at that time, Father Shua Ying, I think spirits existed—Yaushau and Fuatai for instance?'

'It is quite true that Yaushau and Fuatai were then in existence,' said the old man, 'but they are not spirits. Yaushau is the father of Heaven. He created the first human beings, and taught us to plant rice. It was he who sent us fire from heaven.'

The old man was silent, and then added, 'I'm tired. I must smoke opium'.

'We will smoke with you. Then you can tell us some more about our ancestors and our Fuatai.'

'Good,' said Shua Ying. 'First of all Yaushau created a Méo man and a Méo woman. Only afterwards did he carve figures out of a piece of wood: a Chinese, a Thai, and a foreigner. We Méo lived in the most beautiful land. The Chinese were envious. In great hordes they invaded us, stole our land, carried off our women and girls, killed the men. Our Fuatai helped us and drove the Chinese away again and again, but then they succeeded in capturing our Fuatai and in killing him, so that we were at the mercy of the Chinese. Anyone who remained behind became the slave of the oppressor. Whoever could escape did so. It was on this flight that the horses ate our books. Our fathers made for the south. The mountains became less wild and rocky and the forest reached right up their summits. Wherever we found land that we liked we cut down trees, built shacks and planted rice and maize, and yet we could not settle anywhere for long. Either we were driven away or the land was not good.

'One day on their journey our forefathers came to a huge stretch of water. It was not a river like the one down in Pafei. It was much bigger. The Thai called it "Lake". Our fathers had to go through it for there were neither boats nor bridges. They all stepped courageously into the water. It came up to their knees. They went on further. They could not keep their skirts and trousers dry any longer. Bravely they waded on. The water reached the men's girdles. The children were carried, and the group struggled on. The water was cold and reached up to the arms of the adults. Women and children screamed and wailed. They were still not in the middle of the lake. They were seized with fright, thinking they were about to meet a horrible death. They began to cry out: "O spirits of heaven and earth, come and help us! Come spirits, and save us! Henceforth we will bring you sacrifices. We will serve you. Come spirits, come!" Not one was drowned. They all reached the other shore safely. Ever since that day we Méo have been sacrificing to the spirits and are pledged to serve them until our Fuatai comes again and destroys the spirits and all our enemies.'

'Until the Fuatai rises again and comes to help us!' they all cried.

4. *Strange News from the Lowlands*

The dry half of the year came and went, and the village was once more in the middle of the rainy season. The daughter of the Chief's second wife was by now old enough to crawl round the floor of the shack, playing with dogs and pigs and the other naked children, while their baby son went everywhere on Ju's back. In the village it was rumoured that Re wanted to marry a third wife. Mpheng, his first wife, was seldom seen without a tear-stained face, although her loud laughter rang through the whole village as she tried to hide her unhappiness.

Today she was in a good mood and was joking with Re's little sister while they both spun hemp. The mother sat gloomily beside them and worked in silence.

'Here come the Thai!' called the little girl and leapt to the wall where there was a gap through which she could look out.

She was right! Now Mpheng too could hear the little bells of the approaching caravan.

'It's a long time since Thai came,' mumbled the old lady. 'I hope they've brought salt; I haven't a lump left.'

'I don't think the merchants like coming through the wet jungle in the rainy season.'

'I can see them: two, three Thai and two horses, and another horse and . . . and another group of Thai, carrying their baskets on bamboo poles.'

'Who is it?'

'I'm sure they haven't any salt! They are just bringing cloth and I don't want any cloth just now; I want salt! They're not sleeping here, Mpheng, you understand, we are having no merchants in the house while our men are still out hunting.'

'They must be spending the night at Kau's home—see, they are stopping their horses there.'

The women returned to their work. Ju was just bringing

two water buckets into the shack, her baby tied firmly on her back in a gaily embroidered cloth.

'Give me the baby,' demanded Mpheng, 'I'll look after him and then you can cook the rice.'

The sturdy young wife silently untied her baby from her back and handed him over to her mistress.

'Here come our men!' shouted Re's sister triumphantly. 'Look, La and Lautua are carrying a tiger!' The women rushed out to express their admiration in loud voices. Lanang's wife was the only one to stay indoors. She seemed to show no interest in the captured animal.

Mpheng brought Re some dry trousers and he changed in a corner of the shack. Lanang sat by the fire to dry his wet clothes. Tusang had come in with them too.

'Come and pull the splinter out of my toe, wife!' The old woman walked slowly over to Lanang and bent over her husband's swollen foot. The door opened and in the light of the fire they recognised Thai merchants.

'Have you eaten yet?' was their greeting.

'Not yet,' replied Re in Thai.

'Neither have we, and we're very hungry.' With that the merchants sat down by the fire and produced a little bag of rice.

'Have you a pan for our rice?' asked Lom.

'We need our pan ourselves,' grumbled the old woman, who was in the midst of preparing the vegetables.

'Give me one. I'm sure you've got other pans!' Slowly the grandmother brought out a sooty pan and put it down without a word in front of the impudent spokesman. Then she hobbled away, annoyed. The Thai laughed and began to cook their rice. The door creaked again.

'Oh, here you are. Come on, Lien, you can eat with us.'

'I've already had a meal with the Kau family.' Lien sat down on the log beside the other merchants.

'Tusang, have you been hunting too?' he asked.

'No, Lien, I was in Thern with my brother.'

'Did you by any chance go to the priest who can work miracles?'

'Yes I did, but it wasn't any good.'

'Why not?'

'He consulted the spirits, then he looked in my brother's ears, and said in the end that there was nothing he could do.'

'You'll have to take your brother to the foreigners, perhaps they will heal him,' suggested Lom scornfully.

'Which foreigners?' asked the Méo in surprise.

'Oh, don't you know yet—a few days ago two foreigners came to Pakhui, a man with dark hair and glasses. . . .'

'What are glasses?' interrupted someone.

'Two pieces of glass tied in front of the eyes. It's amusing to look at. The foreign woman wears glasses too, but her hair is quite light.'

'Is she so old then that she has grey hair?'

'Her hair isn't grey, it's quite yellow.'

'That's impossible,' exclaimed one of the old men.

'Spirits have yellow hair,' asserted Lanang.

'I've always said,' declared someone else in triumph, 'that this business about foreigners is a fairy tale. They are spirits and not men.'

'The two foreigners have rented a house in our village, and live right next door to us,' said Lien.

'What do the foreigners do in the village?' asked Lanang.

'They have cleaned the house from top to bottom, and even washed it. Two village girls are working for them now. The Mem shows them how they must do the cooking, washing and ironing. Then they have to fetch the water and clean the house each day and go to market in Tak to buy meat, vegetables, and all sorts of other things. Now old Sawat is going every day to teach the foreigners our Thai language.'

The Méo listened in amazement. They couldn't understand why spirits should want to learn Thai, and live in a Thai village. After a while Lien went on:

'The two foreigners speak Thai quite well already, and they can even read and write our language. They like telling about their gods.'

'What are gods?'

'Gods and spirits are the same thing.'

'How many children have the foreigners?'

'None,' laughed Lom scornfully, 'and what's more they are already thirty years old.'

'What, no children? So old already and still no children? That's terrible! Why doesn't the foreigner marry a second wife if the first is barren?'

'Perhaps he'll marry the two servant girls.'

'Do the foreigners' parents and brothers and sisters live in Tak or in Pakhui?'

'No, they live far, far away, somewhere the other side of the great water.'

'Did you hear that? There are two foreigners, without children, without mother or father, brothers or friends. They must be really wicked people, who have been turned out by their relatives!'

All the Méo agreed whole-heartedly, but Lien tried to take the foreigners' part:

'They can't be wicked, because they love children and are kind to us all. When Som was ill they brought him medicine which healed him immediately.'

Excitement, discussion and laughter over these foreigners continued for a long time, but eventually they all went to sleep. Tusang, however, went on thinking over what he had heard. Was it really true that two foreigners had come to Pakhui?

5. *The House on Stilts*

'Here is the house!' Tusang and Tsunshua followed the Thai custom of pouring a tinful of water over their dusty feet before going up the steps.

So this was where the foreigners lived! It was a real Thai house with a tiled roof, wooden walls, a wide door, a kitchen standing apart from the rest, window frames and a large veranda. Everything was clean and tidy. As Tusang and Tsunhua stood in the open doorway, they saw the two foreigners sitting beside their Thai teacher, on high four-legged chairs with a back rest. The visitors stood motionless—so far no one had noticed them. What a strange yellow colour the woman's hair was! What funny things the foreigners wore on the noses! They were reading slowly in Thai. Tusang couldn't understand very much.

'Come on, let's go!' whispered Tsunshua, but it was too late—the foreigner had caught sight of them and was getting up. The Méo boys longed to hurry away, but their feet seemed like lead.

'Come in!' called the foreigner in a cheerful voice, which sounded gruff but inviting. 'Come in, we are very pleased to see you.'

They plucked up courage and went a few steps nearer.

The foreigner took them into a beautiful room with a shiny floor. It contained some more high seats, two tables and a shelf filled with a great many books. Tusang was overawed by them—huge tomes, some thick and others thinner. Whatever was written in them all?

'Please have some tea,' said the foreigner, giving them each a glass, and having some himself.

'This is good tea,' said Tusang appreciatively.

'How much did it cost?' asked Tsunshua.

The foreigner named the price.

'We don't use tea,' they told him.

'What do you drink then?'

'We Méo sometimes drink wine, but usually just water.'

'Are you Méo men?' The question almost shot out.

'Yes we both belong to the great tribe of the Blue Méo.'

'You belong to the Blue Méo tribe? Wait a moment.' He hurried to a table and came back, beaming with pleasure, paper and pencil in hand.

'What kind of book is that?'

'A note book. I write down all sorts of things in it.'

'Why do you do that?'

'Don't you Méo do it, for example, if there is something important you don't want to forget?'

They both doubled up with laughter. At last Tusang said:

'We haven't got any books; no one can write our language. We have no signs that can speak, like the Thai have.'

The foreigner looked as though he didn't believe them. 'Have you no written language at all?'

'The two of us speak and understand Thai very well, but other Méo up in the mountains speak only their own language. We have a good memory and don't need to write things down.'

The foreigner was writing furiously in his little blue book with white pages. Tusang peeped into it. What curious signs they were, almost like the stitches the Méo women worked on their skirts.

'How many Blue Méo are there in Thailand?' asked the foreigner.

'Very many.'

'About how many?'

'O, I don't know; no one knows.'

Tsunshua yawned with boredom. He went to the table and touched all the queer objects lying on it. Here was something interesting! He hurried to the foreigner with a big black book.

'What's in this black book?'

'That is my most precious book, God's book. All sorts of things that are really important for all mankind are written in it.'

'What does "God" mean?'

'He is the King of Thailand,' explained Tusang quickly, 'that's what the Thai call their king.'

'No,' said the foreigner, 'this isn't a book about the Thai king. He's only a man. This is a book about the God of Heaven, who created the earth, the plants and animals, and us men as well.'

The Méo stared at the foreigner, who was talking so enthusiastically. What he was saying was completely new to them. Yaushau created man, but what about the earth? The ancients had said nothing about that. It was possible that the foreigners had a king who could conjure up such things. In his halting Thai the foreigner went on trying to make everything plain to them—his enthusiasm showed how important it was to him. Tusang didn't understand all he said, because his Thai wasn't as good as all that—but he was too proud to ask. The foreigner was talking about someone called Jesu, but that sent the younger men off into peals of laughter.

'Why are you laughing?'

'Because you are always talking about the Lisu. You seem to be very fond of them. Lisu live near us too; their village lies two days' journey to the south. I don't like the Lisu. They're always drunk, and they steal and kill.'

'But I'm not talking about the Lisu,' replied the foreigner, discouraged. 'I'm talking about Jesus. He is the Son of God.'

'We don't know him. We've never heard of anyone called Jesus. Is he a foreigner or a Thai?'

In the next room the lesson had come to an end. The teacher got up and the foreigner hurried to say goodbye to him.

Without a sound one of the servant girls appeared and spread a white cloth on the table.

Spellbound, Tusang's eyes followed the Thai girl round as she gracefully laid the table and brought in the hot midday meal.

'Is that girl married, I wonder?' he whispered to Tsunshua. 'I like the look of her; she's clean, strong and attractive.'

'She's sure to be one of the foreigner's wives.'

'But Lien said he only had one wife, the one over there with the yellow hair. I'll pluck up courage and ask the foreigner to help me, so that I can marry the little slim one, if he doesn't want her himself.'

There was the foreigner back again.

'When are you returning to your village?'

'We're travelling tomorrow with a caravan of Thai traders.'

'Can't you stay here a few more days?'

'No, we will have to go with the traders. Foreigners, come and visit us in our village!'

'How far is your village from here?'

'Only two days' journey.'

'Two days' journey?'

'Yes, we get there through the jungle. But the Thai take three to four days. Our village is the first one you come to, and the others are much farther away.'

The foreigner seemed to be grateful for all the information Tusang was giving him.

'Come back again soon,' he said. 'I should like to know some more. Perhaps you could teach me a few words of your language.'

Tusang smiled. 'No one can learn our Méo language if he has not been born a Méo. We have many sounds which no Thai can pronounce.'

'I know that it's going to be difficult, but our Lord and God will help us, Jesus sent us here because he loves you Méo too. He wants you also to have the chance to hear about Him, so we'll come and see you soon.'

Tusang and his companion hurried away, feeling they had already stayed too long.

'It's funny that the foreigners go to so much trouble to get to know about us,' they said to each other as they walked down the main street of Pakhui. 'They even want to learn our language! We shall have to look out, they might be spies!'

6. *Spirits or Men?*

When Tsunshua and Tusang returned to the village and told the story of their visit to the foreigners in Pakhui, it was the prime topic of conversation for days. But by the time a month had passed, a new excitement had pushed it into the background.

Two men had felled a giant tree in the forest; two days later both were desperately ill: they were lying by the fire with their teeth chattering, and then a few hours later the sweat was pouring off from them. The fever demon had bitten them. Shua Ying, who had been called in, did his best for them. He maintained that they had unwittingly felled the ancestral home of a demon, and the spirit was taking a frightful vengeance. Pigs must be slaughtered without delay. The men of the village hastened to do all that he said in sacrifices and exorcism. But it was no use—by the evening one of the sick men was already dead, and La was lying motionless in the shack.

Tusang was at home, tired of doing nothing. Nshua had gone with his wife and children to Mekong to visit her relatives, and it would be about ten days before they came back. Tusang stretched lazily on the tiger skin that lay spread out under the demon altar. His sister had gone off to the field with his mother to bring home the last of the vegetables. Grandmother Sheng had been in a horrible temper again because her son had taken his wife to Mekong—she had been against it, but this time Nshua had said emphatically: 'It's six years now since my wife saw her parents. This time she is coming with me.'

The fire smoked and the monsoon rain was pattering down again on the leaky leaf roof.

'I'll go and see what's happening in the Chief's shack,' Tusang thought, rolling up the skin and looking for the piece of plastic he had bought once in Pakhui. It was already torn in several places, but even so it afforded better protection than a banana leaf.

'Isn't Re at home?' asked Tusang, arriving at the shack.

'He went to visit La,' said old Lanang. 'Come and sit by the fire, son.'

'Isn't La any better yet?' inquired Tusang.

'No, the spirit is stubborn, and burns with revenge.'

As the two men fell silent, they heard the sound of a distant bell.

'Whoever is coming in this weather?'

Tusang hurried to the corner where he could easily peep through the wide gaps in the wall.

'It's a Thai caravan! They're all wet and covered with mud. I can recognize Lien by his clothes, and I know his horse too.'

As the little group drew near to the Chief's shack, there was wild excitement outside, with the neighbours shouting 'Tlang tue, tlang tua!'

'It's the foreigners!' exclaimed Tusang eagerly. 'No wonder the people are shouting: "the spirits have come".'

Lanang hurried to Tusang's side. Now at last he could see with his own eyes whether these foreigners were spirits or men.

'That one over there,' Tusang pointed, 'who is helping Lien unload his horse, I don't know him, but the shorter one is the foreigner in Pakhui, and standing beside him is his wife.'

Now the door was opening and in came Lien and the tall man. They put down the basket near the wooden platform.

'We've arrived!' said Lien in Thai, by way of greeting.

The tall man said something in Chinese, which Tusang didn't understand, but Lanang had a little conversation with him. Then he turned to Lien: 'You can put the sleeping bag down there on the platform. Push the rice baskets over to the side—here, let me help you, they're heavy.'

Meanwhile the foreigners from Pakhui had also come into the dark shack. Tusang laughed as they both stumbled over the high step and rubbed their eyes.

'You've come!' he greeted them. 'Sit down by the fire!'

'We've come!' answered all three foreigners in Thai.

Tusang thought of the tall clean chairs in Pakhui when he saw the foreigners squat down on the dirty floor.

The neighbours were peeping through the cracks, plucking up courage to come in, as the visitors tried to dry their wet clothes and shoes by the fire. More and more people crowded into the shack. The boldest among them began to ask questions out of curiosity.

'The foreigners don't understand our language,' said Tusang. Then a few men tried to speak to them in Thai. The women, overcoming their fear, came nearer.

'Oh, these spirits have got long noses!'

'How white the woman's skin is!'

'They are so huge!'

They all talked at once. One old grandmother went up to the white woman and felt her big clean hands.

'They are soft and smooth!'

Then the others wanted to feel, too.

When Chief Re returned he was surprised to find so many people in his shack. 'You've come!' he greeted the foreigners politely, and then muttered to Lien in an undertone,

'What have these people come to sell?'

'Nothing,' Lien told him. 'They have all sorts of things to tell us about their gods.'

'How can they do that? They can't speak a word of Méo!'

'They speak Thai and Chinese, though.'

The Chief eyed the strange people sitting by his fire suspiciously. They seemed to be very tired, and their clothes were wet and dirty from the long journey. He still thought it was rather peculiar.

The tall foreigner had put his head in his hands and seemed to be asleep, and the one from Pakhui was sitting beside Lanang holding his little blue book in his left hand. Tusang went up to listen.

'De,' said the foreigners. Everyone laughed.

'De,' repeated Lanang good-humouredly.

'De,' said his pupil.

'It's better, but still not quite right,' thought Tusang. He interrupted and explained in Thai:

'Our Méo language is quite different from Thai. "De" means "hand" but "de" stands for other things too; according to the way the word is said, so the meaning changes.'

The foreigner paid close attention.

'How many tones has your language? The Thai use five different tones.'

'I don't know. You see, there are no Méo books.'

'But I can tell you some of our traditional stories,' Lanang volunteered, and he started straight away:

'Foreigner, I will begin with a poem I composed myself a few days ago. Write it down!' and sure enough he rattled off his poem. Tusang laughed.

'Slowly, please Lanang!' begged the foreigner, trying to write it down.

'Very well, Brother Foreigner, I will say it again quite slowly.'

But he still went too quickly, and it was impossible to write down more than a word every now and again. When a few lines had been recorded Lanang said: 'Now make your paper talk, foreigner!'

He stuttered a few unintelligible words. Everybody laughed. The old people jeered and shook their heads:

'Didn't we say it was impossible to write down our language?'

Lien had got supper ready on the wooden platform. Rice was steaming invitingly, and the vegetables and tinned meat smelled delicious.

'How much does a tin of meat like that cost?' someone enquired. But the foreigners had their hands together and their eyes closed. One of them was saying something quietly in Thai.

'Have they gone to sleep!' asked an old granny.

'No, they are talking to their spirits,' Tusang told her.

Now they began their supper, the shack still crowded with curious onlookers. At last they had had enough, and the foreigner's wife helped Lien to wash up.

The foreigner took a tin out of his kit, and they all three bandaged their bleeding feet and put on dry things.

'They must be doctors,' someone whispered.

'In that case they must have beans for all kinds of illnesses,' said Chief Re, and plucked up courage to ask the foreigners the question in Thai:

'Have you beans for sick people?'

'We haven't many, but we might be able to help.'

'We must have beans that a dying man can swallow.'

'We cannot promise that our medicines will help. Only Jesus can heal. We must trust in Him and believe in Him.'

'Oh, yes, we all believe in your spirits. Come quickly, we want to get to the sick man before he is dead!'

La's motionless form was lying on a bundle of rags. The shack was full of smoke. The foreigners knelt beside the dying man; they felt him and talked to one another. Then the shorter foreigner felt in a pocket and brought out some white pills.

'Have you a spoon?' he asked.

'What does he say?' La's wife muttered to Tusang. 'I don't understand Thai.'

'He wants a spoon,' Tusang interpreted.

'We haven't got one.'

'We have!' said Paure, jumping up and running to fetch it.

'What are these wounds?' the foreigner asked.

'The medicine man made them,' Chief Re told him.

'Why?'

'There is an evil spirit in his chest causing the fever. The medicine man took a red-hot iron and burnt those holes, but even so the spirit won't come out.'

'Jesus alone has power over the spirits,' the foreigner said to them all. 'He came to this earth in order to destroy the power of the spirits. Whoever believes in Jesus need no longer be afraid of the spirits.'

The people chatted excitedly as those who could understand Thai passed the message on to the others. They would have liked to know more. Oh, if only these foreigners could speak their Méo language! Then Paure came back with a bent tin spoon.

'Go and give it a wash—no, not with cold, with hot water!'

A can of water was put on the fire and was soon boiling. The dirty spoon could now be washed.

'How fussy these people are!' thought Tusang, but it was remarkable how clean the spoon became. A white bean was crushed in it, a few drops of water added, and the foreigner's magic potion was ready. Someone opened La's mouth, and the white liquid ran in. The feverish man swallowed it without opening his eyes, and his pale face puckered up, but he was too weak to spit out the bitter medicine.

'We'll come again tomorrow,' said the foreigners, and limped away.

7. The Book from Heaven

It was the day before New Year, and Tusang's mother and sister were pounding the rice for the days of feasting. Ka was cooking.

'Where are you off to now, Tusang?' called his mother as he was hurrying away. 'There isn't enough firewood here, and Nshua can't drag it home all on his own.'

'I'll give him a hand straight away, Mother,' said Tusang, who had just heard the foreigners were at Lanang's. And he was gone.

From the Chief's house came banging and rumbling noises. Re was pounding rice dough with a mallet, in a hollowed tree trunk. Everyone was looking forward to rice cakes. The women were embroidering or pounding rice, while Lanang was busy with a bundle of incense sticks at the demon altar.

'I thought the foreigners were here,' said Tusang, looking round expectantly.

'There's their luggage,' indicated Lanang, nodding towards the board platform.

'But where are they?'

'They've gone to see Nshu Seng's baby daughter—she's very ill.'

As Tusang turned to the door, the foreigners were just coming back, and they greeted each other like old friends. They could speak Méo quite well by now.

'Come on, Teacher,' Tusang said, 'I want to talk to you. There are so many noisy people here, but in my house we can talk in peace. Mem needn't come.'

'I'm coming to see you this evening.' He followed his wife into the shack, and Tusang hurried away.

It was surprising how popular these foreigners had become already. Their white, red and yellow pills partly accounted for it. How quickly La had got well that time, after the foreigners had given him some pills and prayed with him! Everyone had been overjoyed except Kau the medicine man, who was furious, and strongly opposed the opinion of the village that this Jesus was their Fuatai. Tusang didn't know what to make of it. In any case he hoped to do well out of it himself. The Thai told him that the foreigner paid his teacher five hundred *baht* a month. That was a good sum for such easy work!

By now Tusang was standing in front of the door of his shack, and he became aware of the monotonous sound of rice pounding, and of the oaths of his agitated mother. With all speed he disappeared into the forest to look for firewood.

Re's second wife Ju was feeding her pigs when Shuki entered and saw the foreigners. The fair-haired woman was bandaging a little girl's leg. Her husband was sitting with the little blue book beside Lanang, who was having a smoke. Shuki joined them.

'We Méo are so glad that you've come to tell us about our Fuatai,' enthused old Lanang. 'The sick are healed, the poor become rich and no one will die any more.'

'But brother Lanang, first we have to believe in this Jesus. We must let Him save us from the power of the demons and of evil.'

Shuki was amazed to hear how the foreigner's Méo had improved. It was really quite intelligible now. Even his fair-haired wife was talking to the people in their mother tongue.

Lanang was giving some more information about the Fuatai and in the end the foreigner pulled a black book out of his brown haversack. Shuki saw that it contained Thai letters, and he moved over eagerly to look. The white man began to read from it slowly, trying to translate, sentence by sentence, into the Méo language. He did not get on very well. Shuki helped him to correct the mistakes, but in many cases he didn't know what the Thai word meant.

'The Thai in this book is quite different from the language the traders speak,' admitted Shuki.

'I don't understand a word of it!' said Lanang, discouraged.

'I must go home,' Shuki said. 'Tomorrow I'll come and teach you some more of our language, Brother Foreigner. Goodnight to you both.'

'Wait Shuki, I'll come a little way with you.' The foreigner got up and disappeared with him into the darkness.

'Teacher, I believe in this Jesus.' Shuki said earnestly to him as they walked through the village. 'I want to help you to learn our language quickly. We all long to hear about our Fuatai, Jesus—up till now we didn't even know he was called Jesus. Your Jesus is stronger than the evil spirits, so we all want this Jesus. But it's essential that you get a thorough grasp of our language; then we'll all believe, and honour you. I'll help you to set up a school so that we can all learn to read—that will be splendid. How much money will you give me for this?'

The foreigner didn't say anything for a long time. They both walked on in the pitch dark night. At last he began:

'I'm very pleased to hear you say that you believe in Jesus, Brother Shuki. I know too that it is the duty of my wife and myself to get a good grasp of your beautiful Méo language. I'm thankful that you are willing to help me in this. I very much want to tell you more about this Jesus, and I will pay you for the time you spend in teaching me. But I must emphasize one thing—it's a great privilege to know about Jesus and to be able to tell others about Him. Everyone who truly believes in Him must do his part, not for money, but out of love and thankfulness. You see, my wife and I came to you to help you. How much do we ask for when we bind up festering wounds? Nothing. We sell the pills at the price we paid for them. How much do we ask for to pull out a tooth? Nothing. What do you have to pay when we tell you about Jesus for hours on end? You know very well that we do it all for nothing.'

Shuki listened in silence. He was quite right, of course. That was why they were so fond of these two, because they were so different from the grasping Thai.

'But who gives you the money for food and clothes,' he asked, 'and for paying for Lien's pack-horses? Does Jesus send you money down from heaven?'

'No, but in our country there are many people who love Jesus and believe in Him. They pray for us and send us money so that we can live and work here. Once there are people here in this village who really believe in Jesus, they'll want to help in the same way, to spread the news of Jesus to other villages. In China that's what the Lisu. . . .'

'The Lisu! Do those robbers believe in Jesus too? The Lisu don't know anything about Jesus. They sacrifice to the spirits just like we Méo do.'

'In China there are many Lisu who believe in Jesus and have burnt their spirit altars. . . .'

'What? They . . . they burnt . . . their spirit altars?'

'Yes,' replied the foreigner calmly, 'the man who believes in Jesus doesn't want to have any more to do with the spirits.'

The two of them walked on and on, and the foreigner talked and talked. The moon had risen meanwhile, and there was bustling activity in every shack. Tomorrow a new year would begin. Everyone would worship his ancestors and sacrifice to the spirits.

It was broad daylight.

Lanang was pushing incense sticks into the mud floor of the shack. New paper strips were already adorning the altar. The next thing was to offer the blood sacrifices. As hens and pigs were slaughtered Lanang sang a quiet rhythmical accompaniment. The two foreigners sat on the floor by the fire and watched all that was going on in silence.

'Why are you so sad?' asked Lanang suddenly. 'We are celebrating our one and only festival today, and that's why everyone is gay. We are going to drink wine, smoke opium, play ball with the girls, and spend the night with them in the forest.'

'We are sad because you are grieving the Lord Jesus.'

'How are we grieving our Fuatai Jesus?' The old man looked at the foreigners in astonishment.

'Because you sacrifice to the spirits and revere the ancestors, but you are not willing to obey our Lord Jesus.'

Meanwhile Tusang had come in. Without saying a word

he sat down beside the white couple. Lanang was saying in a firm voice:

'But, Brother Foreigner, don't be so sad. We do all believe in Jesus and worship Him. Jesus is higher than the sky; Fuatai is greater than all spirits. Don't be afraid, we have our Fuatai Jesus!'

'But if you do believe in Jesus how can you bring these sacrifices and do all that goes with them?'

'Don't worry, Brother,' the old man put his arm round his friend's shoulders. 'We only do that because it's the custom. We have to do it because our forefathers told us to. It's the way of the tribe. You foreigners have books and so you don't do these things. But up till now we haven't had any books, and until we have, we Méo are pledged to serve the spirits and our ancestors. That's why we serve the Fuatai Jesus, but serve the spirits as well. As soon as we have books. . . . Stay with us, Foreigner, and I'll help you to write books!'

Lanang got up and went to the altar, where he continued the ritual, muttering as he did so. Tusang pulled up nearer to the foreigner and said to him quietly,

'Yesterday I was asking too much. I want to help you learn the language, and you can give me what you think best. Agreed?'

The foreigners exchanged glances, sad that both Shuki and Tusang were out for what they could get. Then the husband said: 'Right, we will talk about that later. I should like to know what the different objects you use in offering sacrifices are called.'

'I'll teach you. Come on, let's go up to the altar.'

It must have been far on in the night, and in the village quietness had descended at last after feverish activity. Tusang was lying in his narrow room and staring out into the darkness. It was strange that the foreigner insisted so stubbornly on his own way in money matters. As far as other things went he was easy-going and got on with the Méo as no one else, Thai or Chinese, had ever done. But it was a foolish idea that later on the Méo here who became Christians should support their own teacher, and give their produce and help in spreading the Jesus religion. The affairs of the Christians were not to be decided by the foreigner alone, he said, but all were to be able to have their say. The foreigner didn't realize that it was he the people were following. If he were to assert that he was the Fuatai, all the Méo would worship him and make him their supreme chief.

'He's a blockhead not to ask for that! He's not satisfied that all the Méo intend to believe in Jesus, he's asking us to destroy our spirit altars as well. Well, he'll wait a long time for that! No Méo will ever do it. It's a pity, for in many ways I like this new religion. I wonder how it's all going to end?'

8. *The House on the Hill of the Spirits*

'Come on Tusang, it's time you were up! We're going to build the foreigners' house today.' Was it morning already? Half asleep he rubbed his eyes. The light of the new day was filtering through the gaps in the walls and the women were busy about the shack.

Soon Tusang was standing with his bush knife in the Chief's house, where a big crowd was already waiting. The foreigner was standing ready too, with his curious knife. His fair-haired wife was dropping red medicine into La's eyes.

'Where is your house to stand?' asked Lanang.

'I will show you the place straight away.'

Everyone followed Lanang and the foreigner out into the burning sun.

'Here on this little hill,' he pointed out, 'right by Lautua's house.'

Tusang stared at the foreigner from the side, and then looked round at the group of Méo. They were all speechless. Finally Lanang coughed a few times and said:

'Dear Teacher, we will build your house in a much better place. Look, up here.'

'But the foreigner replied: 'My wife and I think this hill is excellent. Here we are in the middle of the village, and everyone can come quickly to us. If you agree, we'll build our house here.'

'Of course our teacher can have his house wherever he likes,' Lanang said uneasily, 'but it is a very evil place here. No, we can't possibly build your house here.' The old man looked round for someone to help him. Tusang would gladly have explained why no shack could be situated there, but the elderly and influential were standing by, so he kept quiet.

It was Shuki who went up to the foreigner and said, earnestly,

'Teacher, we can't build a house here because this is

where the spirits dwell.' Now it was out. Tusang watched the foreigner closely, but he could see no terror in his face. Calmly he explained: 'My wife and I are not afraid of the spirits. Jesus is with us, and He is far more powerful than all spirits and powers of darkness. We will gladly live here as long as you are not afraid to build here. It will be a good thing, because then you will be able to see that the spirits cannot harm us.'

The Méo huddled together for a discussion—some laughed but others were looking very serious.

'Well,' said Lanang, 'we're not afraid to build your house here, but we just want to warn you. We should be very sorry if you met with some disaster. We want to keep you with us for ever.' There were tears in his eyes and his voice trembled with emotion.

'Very well.' The foreigner smiled kindly. 'It's very good of you to be so concerned for us, but you needn't have any fear of building here. We'll put our trust in the Lord Jesus and ask Him that this may be a house of blessing.'

At that Lanang said, 'Let's begin. It's a very good site, and it's good that it's so near to my house'.

'Thank you very much, dear friends: now we will make a start with the building in the name of Jesus.' He put his hands together and spoke to Jesus as if He were standing beside him. Tusang shut his eyes unintentionally for a moment, and then opened them again, embarrassed. Lanang and Shuki were standing right by the foreigner, as if they were teachers too. Now the foreigner was ready, however, and the work began. One group went to fell trees, and Shuki directed the men who were going to level the site. Tusang and Tsunshua and the other young men started on the long walk to cut the leaves of the fan palms.

The sun was high in the heavens by the time they came back to the building site with huge bundles.

'The house is up already!' exclaimed Tsunshua in amazement.

'It's a big house for only two people.'

'The foreigners need big houses because they have more possessions than we do.'

In the evening it was raining, but the following day brought renewed sunshine. Lanang called the people together again after he had smoked his morning opium.

'Is the foreigner going to kill a pig for us and provide wine all round?' Tsunshua asked his friend.

'Certainly not,' replied Tusang. 'The foreigners haven't any pigs and they don't drink wine.'

'What will he give us then at the house warming?'

'Nothing. You know quite well that we promised to build the house for nothing. In exchange they will stay here to teach and help us.'

By this time they had reached the building site, where a dozen fellows were sitting on the roof tying leaves on to the bamboo framework. Tusang clambered up quickly and asked for leaves to be thrown up to him too. In the sky dark clouds were gathering from the west. They all worked hard, for in a short time the tropical rain would be falling again.

By the time they felt the first drops the shack was roofed in and the walls were complete. Only the opening for the door remained uncovered. Of course, there were no windows.

'Tomorrow we'll make the sleeping platform; then you can move in,' Lanang told them. Then everyone went home except Tusang and Tsunshua who stayed with the foreigner until his wife joined him.

'We'll come tomorrow and help you,' they told him.

'Thank you, Tusang; that's fine.'

'How do you like the house?'

'We like it very much, and we're so glad to be able to come and live among you.'

'Tusang, Tsunshua! Where are you?'

'It's La. Come on, let's go with him.'

Tusang ran after his friend. At the door he stopped and looked back. The foreigners were tired and were leaning against the wall. The floor was wet and sticky. There were a thousand gaps in the walls, and rain was dripping through the holes in the roof. It was gloomy, wet and lonely. How long would the foreigners hold out?

9. *Books and Discs that speak our Language*

'I'm sorry, but my husband is ill and cannot possibly work,' the fair-haired woman told Tusang.

'What's the matter with him?'

'He's feverish and his tonsils are swollen.' The foreigner coughed at that moment on the other side of the bamboo wall.

'Teacher, can't you help us to write the book of John today?' Tusang shouted. 'Tomorrow I'll have to go to the opium field for a few days.'

'Unfortunately I can't get up. You write it on your own. Shuki is sure to come too.'

'But there's so much I don't understand.' He had tried the day before to translate the fifteenth chapter, but he scarcely understood a word of it. It was much more difficult than the book of Mark.

The door creaked and in walked Lanang. He put the dried melon-skin of rice down on the table cloth, greeted the white woman and Tusang, and looked round the shack.

'Where's our teacher?'

'In bed. He's ill.'

'Ill? I thought anyone who believed in Jesus would never be ill any more. Come on, Tusang, let's pray that Jesus will heal our good teacher. Heaven and earth will have pity on him. Our ancestors will help to expel the sickness demon.'

Lanang walked to the door and shouted loudly in all directions. Satisfied, he came back into the shack.

'Don't be afraid, the teacher will get better now. Here's some rice for the pills you gave me yesterday.'

The door creaked again. This time it was Shuki with his youngest child.

'Is the teacher at home?' he asked.

'He's ill and staying in bed today,' said Tusang, forestalling the foreigner's wife.

'Well then, let's go on translating in the book of John.'

Shuki sat on the teacher's chair. Tusang sat on the box

nearby. Lanang looked curiously over the shoulders of the other two.

'What does that mean?' Lanang enquired, and pointed at a place in the book.

'I don't know,' replied Tusang.

'What is a vine, Teacher?' called Shuki through the thin wall. The foreigner coughed and then began to describe a foreign plant. They all looked puzzled.

'What are we to call this plant in our language?'

It was very hard work.

Next day Tusang and his family went off to the opium fields to work there for a few days. Other families were there too, and the fire was smoking in the shelter as Tsunshua squatted beside Tusang to discuss the latest news.

'When did she do it?'

'Three days ago—my sister saw it herself. Wang was drawing water from the stream and the foreign woman was standing by her to do her washing. Wang talked about believing in Jesus. Then the fair-haired woman said: "If you have such a sure faith in Jesus, why do you still wear these lifestrings round your arm?" Wang was horrified, but in the end she had to admit that these strings weren't in keeping with the faith in Jesus. The following day the strings had disappeared, and her daughter Fong is no longer wearing any life strings either.'

'Whatever did Lateng say?'

'Lateng didn't oppose her. He still wears them himself, but he'd like to remove them. They are worthless, he says, and Jesus is able to protect.'

'How frightful! Now Wang is sure to die.' When the women heard this news they gasped with horror. Grandmother Sheng muttered a magic spell to protect her house from the wrath of the spirits.

The next day it only rained a little, so Tusang and his family could put in a good day's work. Soon all the poppy seed was in the earth and it could germinate and grow quickly in the damp soil.

'Who's that coming up the mountain?' Nshua called out suddenly.

'It's Paure! What does he want here?'

By now the boy was standing before them, panting out his message.

'Tusang, come to the village quickly! The foreigners are asking for you. They can't make the talking disc without you.'

'What's that you're saying about talking discs?'

'Yesterday evening three foreigners came and are living with our teacher. One is terribly tall. They have brought with them a box and they want to make talking discs with it: you know, the kind the foreigners have in the Thai language. But now they want to make discs that speak *our* language. Yesterday La helped, but it didn't work very well. And Shuki tried too, but because he has no teeth the discs don't speak clearly. The teacher said that Tusang must make these discs, otherwise they won't be any good.'

Grandmother Sheng gave Paure a black look and cursed aloud. Tusang on the other hand was flattered. Of course the others couldn't do it! He was extremely curious to know how such discs could be made to speak Méo while they were still turning round in the foreigner's box.

'How does it work?' he asked Paure.

'The teacher sits on a chair and holds a big piece of paper in front of him. He told me that something's written on it in the English language. Then he translates a few words into our language, and La says them fluently and clearly while the tall foreigner raises his finger, and the teacher holds a shiny thing in front of La's mouth. The tall man presses a button and the red box makes a buzzing noise. A wheel turns round, and when it's turned back the tape talks in our language!'

Everyone was listening with amazement. The old grandmother was the only one who did not want to know anything about the foreigners' magic.

'Well, Paure, I'll come with you straight away.'

'Tusang, you stay here. Tusang. . . .' But he'd already gone.

'What will be the end of all this?' said his brother Nshua under his breath.

The night was dark, and a few lights were flickering in the foreigners' shack. Tusang was almost stifled in his corner, because the whole village seemed to be present—many who hadn't been able to find room in the shack were standing outside.

'I didn't know there were so many foreigners,' someone said. Tusang smiled at his own superior knowledge. He knew that there were even more foreigners than these five, indeed far more than all Thai and Méo and Lisu put together.

Now the teacher was praying. Tusang looked round. Most of the Méo kept their eyes open, and a few went on chattering. The foreigners kept their eyes closed and their hands together. A few Méo copied them—it was easy to see who often went to the foreigners. Now the prayer had ended, and Tusang could scarcely wait to hear his voice come out of the box. The people were shouting with excitement, though a few were afraid. At last it was quiet enough to be able to hear, and the foreigner started the machine. The whole village listened in stunned silence.

'Those are Méo words!'

'It's our language!'

'What is said is true!'

'Away with the altars! Away with the spirits! Jesus is stronger. We want Jesus!' they shouted as they began to understand the message.

The disc went on talking, and then the preacher and his wife spoke to the big crowd.

'Tomorrow I will burn my altar!' announced Lanang in a loud voice. I'm not afraid of the spirits.'

Shuki too was eager to persuade everyone.

Tusang was too hot. He pushed his way through the throng to the door, and Tsunshua followed him.

'Re isn't back yet, is he?'

'No; I wonder what he'll say to it?'

'If Re burns the altar, so will I.'

Now the people were coming out of the shack and hurrying off home with flares and torches, excited and happy. There was Kau hobbling away—what did the magician really think? Almost all the Méo had gone. Tsunshua and Tusang peeped through the walls, and saw Lateng sitting next to the teacher; they were talking eagerly together. Now they were both praying. The teacher got up and went over to the little medicine box, and came back with a pair of scissors. He handed them to Lateng, who cut his life-strings! Tusang held his breath. The strings fell from his right arm too, and Lateng, laughing, threw them into the fire. Again the teacher and Lateng prayed.

'Did you see?' Tsunshua whispered.

Tusang only nodded. He couldn't believe his eyes. He was waiting to see how the spirits would destroy the offender. But it didn't seem as if anything was going to happen.

'Let's go home.'

The foreigners were there for four days. Tusang had been able to make five discs and La three. All the Méo were enthusiastic now over the Jesus religion, and some were pressing for an immediate burning of the spirit altars. But nobody wanted to be the first to do it. Even Lanang had burnt his life-strings, but he wouldn't burn his altar while his son was away.

'Tusang! Tusang!' shouted Tsunshua, 'there are White Méo at the foreigners' house!'

'What do they want?'

'Pills, perhaps.'

'Come on. Let's go and see.'

The foreigner was in his shack, chatting happily to the White Méo visitors. Tusang smiled because he noticed how little they understood one another—the White Méo dialect was quite different from the Blue Méo which the foreigners were learning. But they managed all the same.

Lanang and Shuki and the others were there, telling the visitors about Jesus. Tusang sat beside them, while Tsunshua stood watching at the door.

The White Méo from their distant village were glad to

hear the news they were told. Their eyes shone and they kept on expressing their joy.

'They are different from us,' thought Tusang. 'They talk a lot and say things to please, but they think the opposite in their hearts. We Blue Méo don't express our emotions quickly, but on the other hand we are dependable and not fickle.'

The visitors had brought gifts of chickens, rice, vegetables and even silver. What were they expecting in return? Perhaps they wanted to steal the foreigner away to their village.

'Tusang, come on,' muttered Tsunshua in his ear. 'I must go home. Father doesn't like me to be here.' The two friends went off unnoticed.

The White Méo stayed at the foreigners' house for three days. Tusang didn't go over there any more, but the whole village was in an uproar. Work in the fields was neglected. Young and old were discussing the swing of opinion that was imminent. Every day life-strings were burnt and bones and amulets thrown away. Eventually Tusang destroyed his life-strings too, in spite of his mother's protests.

Then one day Tsunshua burst in with the news:

'The White Méo have gone now, but there was plenty of noise in the foreigners' house last night.'

'Who was there then?'

'As well as the White Méo, there were Lanang and Kau and Shuki and Lateng and Wang. . . .'

'What were they doing? why wasn't I invited?' thought Tusang resentfully. Lanang and Shuki were there, that was understandable, but why Lateng and his wife? They were neither rich nor intelligent.

'What were they doing? You should have seen how many chickens they killed, as if it had been New Year! They sat together there almost the whole night. When the foreigner had prayed the prayer before the meal, one after another prayed too, each more loudly and at greater length than the one before. In between the teacher was teaching them about Jesus. After the meal all the White Méo men cut off their life-strings, and knelt and prayed. They begged the foreigner to come to them soon and to help them burn their altars. They all wanted to believe in Jesus and give up spirit worship. But Lanang and Shuki protested and said: "No, we can't agree to that! They must help here first. As soon as Re is back all our demon altars will be burnt and we shall worship only Jesus. We're going to learn to read, too." It was decided that Shuki would go with the foreigners to the White Méo village in a fortnight's time.'

It all seemed like a dream to Tusang. It was obviously high time he came out on the side of the foreigners—but he still wasn't sure what the Chief would say about it all.

'But what was Kau doing there?' he asked Tsunshua.

'He's all on fire for the Jesus religion now! He says he'll burn his altar at New Year.'

'What does your father think about it? Is he still against it?'

'Father says we should wait and hear what the Chief thinks.'

'And what about you, Tsunshua?'

'We Méo never do anything without our Chief, do we?' Tsunshua replied, 'and we always act together, as brothers. This is such an important matter that it needs to be thought over very thoroughly. One man alone can't do anything. If we're all in favour and the Chief says, "Burn", *then* we shall burn our altars.'

'Well said!' Tusang looked thoughtfully into the fire. That's what everyone would think. No one would be able to make any change, not even the foreigner. That was the custom of the Méo, and that was how it would always remain.

10. The Great Village Meeting

A new morning had dawned over the jungle village. Tusang set off for the Chief's shack while it was still early. Had Re come home?

Already the big shack was full of men. There by the centre pole sat Re, with his cousin Gi, chief of another village, and old Chief Sing beside him. They had both come to help the village make this vital decision. Lanang was sitting by the fire and staring absent-mindedly into the embers, looking as though he might have drunk too much wine. The discussion was heated, and faces were red. Now Sing with his wider knowledge of the world outside the village, was beginning to speak.

'Down in Pafei the Thai are also talking about this new religion, but not one of them has become a Jesus man. In the town of Tak a few foreigners have been preaching about this Jesus for some years. Have people there been convinced? Not a single one! They say the foreigners want to incite us to rebellion against the Thai. They want to make us into soldiers and then we shall have to fight against the Thai.'

'That's all right, we'll gladly help the foreigners against the Thai!' laughed a few.

But Sing went on with his warning: 'What are a few foreigners? We are the ones who have to live in the Thai's land and be dependent on them. The head man in Pafei said to me, "If you become Jesus people you will not be allowed to live in Thailand any longer; you can go and live in the foreigners' land".'

Fear was reflected on every face. Sing continued: 'No doubt it is right to believe in this Jesus. I do myself. Indeed, I have seen how effective the prayers and pills of the foreigner are. But why burn the altars? Why give up our sacred customs?'

Courageously old Lanang spoke up: 'Our Fuatai Jesus is

stronger than the spirits, and He hates them. We must choose between them. I am in favour of burning the altars.'

Re still said nothing. And now Chief Gi came forward.

'My dear brothers, listen to me. You have the privilege of having the two foreigners in your village. You can go and see them every day and hear more about their religion. You can buy good medicines here for very little. You have the foreigners whenever you need them to stand by you with help and advice. Just think! There are countless other Méo villages which know nothing of these things. These Méo are our brothers. They have the same ancestors, they offer sacrifices to the same spirits as we do. And now you want to accept this Jesus teaching? What are you thinking of? The other villages will not do so. You haven't begun to think what is involved, so listen to reason! You can't do anything without the Méo everywhere else having to know about it. I suggest that you continue to sacrifice to the spirits and honour them, and at the same time pray quietly to this Fuatai Jesus! Learn as much as you can about him, but wait until all Méo are of one mind before you become Jesus people!'

Nshu Seng said: 'When we Méo believe in Jesus we can pray to Him, and He helps us, even if the foreigner is not here.'

'We cannot pray; we have no books,' objected Gi.

'My wife can pray very well,' retorted Nshu Seng. 'The foreign woman taught her. When our baby was ill my wife put her hands together and shut her eyes, and asked Jesus to heal the child. She got better.'

Lively discussion followed. A few men went out of the room. Finally Sing cleared his throat and said:

'None of this worries me at all, nor am I afraid of the spirits' vengeance. The thought that troubles me very much is that as long as our brothers in other villages still pray to the spirits we Jesus people won't be able to get our children married. Just imagine what it will be like. They will never give us their children unless we offer the necessary sacrifices. I believe Chief Gi has spoken wisely. When the foreigners have spread their doctrine in all the villages, and the Méo everywhere are ready to burn their altars, then we will do so too. Meanwhile let us be glad that the foreigners live with us to teach us and to heal our diseases, but not provoke our spirits or change our sacred customs.'

'I agree with Chief Sing and Chief Gi,' said Re. 'Thank you, brothers, for coming. Now let's have a drink of wine together.'

11. The Turning Point

A few days later, when the Méo of Yellow Creek were rejoicing because the rice had grown so big, the discussion was resumed at the Chief's house. This time the foreigner was to be present.

As Tusang hurried in he looked round for Chief Sing, but couldn't see him anywhere. Presumably he had considered his opium pipe much more important than the discussion! He had given his opinion, anyway, and didn't intend to change it. But the people wanted him to appear, so Lautua went to fetch him, as the foreigner opened his black book and read from it. Then he got up and spoke with voice and eyes full of earnestness. Sing and Lautua appeared. The conversation went backwards and forwards.

Suddenly Nshu Seng jumped up and said in a loud voice:

'For a long time you have been saying that the altars should be burnt and yet no one dares to do it. Either we believe in Jesus or we don't! My wife and I believe, and we have decided to burn our altar!'

Lanang came forward, looking worried. 'We must wait until our brothers in the other villages believe.' Then the meeting erupted into chaos, with passionate talking and shouting making it impossible to follow what was happening. Tusang watched young Chief Re, who was sitting by the fire with a mocking smile on his face. At last he stood up, and the room quietened to hear him.

'What is this wonderful Jesus always saying to you?' he sneered. 'Who has seen Him? I haven't. Perhaps the foreigner has deceived us. The Thai don't believe in Jesus, do they? If we no longer want our spirits, why don't we become Buddhists like the Thai?'

A few men laughed and Sing shouted out: 'You know what I think. Why do a few of you suddenly have to start agitating about it—can't you wait until we take the step together? If you really can't wait, all right, burn your altars!'

'We do not want to do anything against the wishes of our brothers,' said Lautua. 'Let's decide together whether to burn our altars now or not!'

'But not every family is represented. We'll call all the men together another time and decide,' said Re.

'It's not a good thing to keep putting it off,' warned La.

Then the foreigner got up slowly and walked into the middle of the crowded shack. He warned the Méo forcefully not to treat such an important matter lightly. He talked fluently for a long time.

'All right, let Shuki be the first to burn his altar!' shouted Re, and others laughed and clapped.

'Yes. Shuki should be the first. He knows more about Jesus than the rest of us.'

'But Shuki isn't at home.'

'He told his wife to burn his altar if we did it while he was away.'

'Ha! Ha! Then Shuki's wife shall be the first!' decided the Chief. While this was going on Lanang had been cooking chicken and now he called the people to him: 'Let's ask the bones of this chicken.'

Everyone wanted to see how the sign would turn out.

'The bones are very favourable towards the Jesus religion,' Lanang decided. He went up to the foreigner and patted him on the shoulder in a fatherly way.

'Don't worry, teacher. Everything's all right. In two or three days we shall burn our altars. In two or three months we shall all be like you and worship only Jesus.' That seemed to be the end of the matter, and the meeting was beginning to break up.

But suddenly Lateng shouted out:

'Brothers, if you don't want to burn tonight, I will dare to do it alone. Come on, teacher, let's go to my house.'

The men looked at one another horrified. Lautua recovered first and cried: 'I will burn too!'

'So will I,' announced Nshu Seng.

A small group left the shack with the foreigner, and the others sat on, whispering. Tusang would have liked to go out too, but he dared not. Something tremendous had happened, something that had never happened before. Tusang looked apprehensively at the door—would the spirits destroy the whole village now? They could all hear the strange sounds of a Jesus song in the distance. Tusang got up slowly and went to the door, and others followed him to where they could peep into Lateng's shack through the cracks in the wall. They saw Lateng, Wang and their daughter, Fong, kneeling beside the foreigners, praying. When Lateng had finished his wife began, and then their daughter prayed too. They all said much the same:

'Fuatai Jesus, we believe in you. Come into my heart now and dwell in our house. We don't want to be slaves of the spirits any longer. We just want to live to serve you. Fuatai Jesus, wash my heart white with your blood. Fuatai Jesus, protect me and bless me. Amen.'

Now they were getting up and Lateng was going with the foreigner to the altar. The teacher read something out of the black book. Then Lateng tore the altar away, and the ancestors' plaque with the blood and the chicken feathers. He threw it all into the fire. Tusang held his breath. He saw Lateng tremble, and Wang fell on her knees and grasped the hands of the foreign woman:

'Will it be all right?'

Tusang couldn't bear to watch any longer. His heart was beating as if it would burst, and he ran home as quickly as he could.

12. The New Trail

'Did you have a good night, Lateng?'

'Splendid. We had only pleasant dreams, didn't we, Wang?'

'Jesus is mighty,' said Wang. 'I'm so glad that we don't have the spirits any longer.'

'Where's Fong?' Tusang went on to ask.

'At the teacher's to learn to read, replied her mother proudly. 'He's started giving lessons every day. Nshu Seng's boys are learning, too.'

'What sort of books are they studying, Thai or foreign?'

'Oh no, he's teaching them from the Jesus book in our language!'

Tusang hurried to the teacher's house to see for himself. The fire was smoking under the big kettle, and nearby the teacher was squatting beside the three Méo children, writing with his forefinger on the ash-covered floor.

'We're learning to read and write,' he explained. 'This is an A here. Look, Tusang, how nicely Neng and Fong can write.'

Tusang bent down to look at the letters, and then sat comfortably by the fire to watch and listen. The children were learning a verse now:

'Jesu le ntshang ntsua be le tse hu hu le.' ('The blood of Jesus cleanses us from all sin.')

After that they sang: 'Lu ku lu sha. . . .' ('Come into my heart. . . .')

Then the foreigner prayed, and the children ran off happily, bumping into Nshu Seng in the doorway.

'Have you learned a lot?' he asked his boys, and then came in and said to the foreigner, 'Teacher, let's pray that they will soon be able to read the Jesus book'.

Tusang put his hands together with the others, and stayed quiet while they prayed, but he didn't join in. The door creaked, and La appeared with a beaming Lateng. After they had greeted each other La said,

'Teacher, we've decided to burn our altar today. Please come over with your wife. We don't want to serve the spirits any longer—we want to serve Jesus. Please come quickly!'

'That's wonderful!' said the teacher. 'Let's call the brothers and sisters who believe in Jesus already. They must come too.' Lateng hurried away happily to fetch them, while the teacher went on talking to La.

'I'm so glad that you and your family want to believe in Jesus. It won't be easy, but the Lord Jesus will help you. Trust Him completely and always obey Him.'

Tusang, still sitting quietly in his corner, was amazed when the door opened yet again, and an old grandmother came in.

'Teacher, I want to burn my ancestral plaque and to become a child of God too. My two daughters also want to believe. Please come quickly and help us to burn it all.'

'Wait a minute, Grandmother!' said the teacher. 'We'll gladly come to your house, but first we must go and burn at Brother La's; then we'll come straight over to you. We're very glad, dear sister, that now you also want to step out openly on the narrow trail.'

'Tusang, when are you burning?' asked Nshu Seng.

'I should like to but Mother won't,' he replied. 'And my brother Nshua also thinks we should wait for the Chief.'

'Jesus is our Chief. We must obey His voice.'

Tusang felt out of it and wished he had never come.

'I'm going to Lanang's to see if the Thai are there,' he muttered, and disappeared quickly. 'It's all so new, so completely contrary to our customs,' he thought as he ran through the village. 'Now La and Grandmother Seng Shua want to accept the Jesus religion too! It's a pity the Chief doesn't take the new trail—then everyone would certainly follow. Anyway it's a good thing I can hide behind my mother and brother!'

Tusang had spent several days in the opium field and felt

out of touch. He wondered what had happened while he was away. As he came up by the stream he heard several women chattering excitedly together, and went to talk to them.

'Lanang burnt his altar today!' they told him, all talking at once.

'Whatever did Chief Re say to that?'

'Re was there too, with the rest of the family! He knelt with the others and prayed and sang.'

Tusang didn't really believe them and went straight to the Chief's shack. As soon as he went in he saw that it was true. Where the huge altar had hung, a poster bore witness to the new faith. The red cloth over the door had disappeared, and so had the blood-smeared paper with the chicken feathers. Lanang was lying on the platform smoking opium with two Thai traders.

'Come on, Tusang, have a smoke with us,' invited the old man. Tusang declined, but he sat down with them and asked:

'Lanang, have you burnt your altar too, now?'

'Yes, Tusang, Lanang no longer serves the spirits. I and all my children and grandchildren now serve the Fuatai Jesus. Our Fuatai is as high as heaven. . . .'

'But why do you still smoke opium? I thought that when anyone started out on the new trail he wasn't allowed to smoke opium any more.'

'The important thing is that Jesus has saved us, and we have life that never ends. I'm an old man, I can't break with opium now. But it's good for the younger ones not to smoke any more.'

The women were going to the door, and Lanang's wife called to him, 'We're going to the foreigner's wife. They have a meeting there every evening'. Tusang, consumed with curiosity, followed the women.

The foreigners' house was already full of men, women and children. The eleven families which had believed in Jesus were well represented, and other Méo and two Thai were present. The teacher's wife was playing the concertina, and a few brave folk were trying to sing with her. Tusang didn't know the song.

'The foreigner has written it for us today,' said Paure proudly. 'Don't you like it?'

'Yes, I should like to learn it.'

Nshu Seng's wife got up to rock the baby, whom she was carrying on her back. The little girl had been crying miserably, but now she stopped.

The teacher was telling them about Jesus and a man called Nicodemus. Tusang knew the story—he'd helped to translate it a few months before—but it was difficult to understand the meaning. As the teacher talked, Tusang understood all sorts of things that had seemed a riddle to him before.

When the preaching was over the foreigner prayed first, then many of the Jesus folk. Tusang felt uncomfortable. He went out with a few other young men.

'I can't understand how such a great change has taken place,' he said to Tsunshua. 'I don't recognize Lateng and La any more.'

'You know, Tusang,' his friend said, 'I think it's because they've left the old way and started on a new way.'

'Yes, the narrow way,' Tusang replied soberly.

13. Is the New Trail too Steep?

'Tusang, the Chief's come back from Rock Caves. Come on, let's go and visit him.' Tusang hurriedly put his hatchet down and accompanied Tsunshua.

'Does anyone know when the foreigners are coming back?'

'They said they wanted to go to Chiengmai to print Méo books, but they've been away ten days already.'

'Everyone's saying they won't be back!'

There was a lot of noise in the Chief's shack. Everyone was trying to push in and hear what Re had to tell.

'We were three days at Rongkau's,' he started off. 'And I was able to ask a lot of questions about this new Jesus teaching.'

'Does he actually know something about it?' interrupted a voice from the back.

'Oh yes! He told us how he'd seen foreigners in Laos; they used to wear long black clothes and tell the people about Jesus.'

'But our foreigners don't wear long black clothes!' objected Lateng.

'And these men taught the children to read,' he went on. 'But what happened? When the children went to live with them in the big town to study the foreigners murdered the children. They cut them up into little pieces and made them into tinned meat!'

'Horrible!' the women shrieked, and the men cursed.

'Is that a fact?' asked Nshu Seng.

'We wouldn't have believed it,' continued Re, 'but Rongkau swore he'd seen it with his own eyes. He even said: "Let the spirits punish me if I'm not telling the truth." And he pointed out to us that our foreigners here have the same thing in mind. As soon as we have all set out on their Jesus way and the children are learning in their home, they will murder them!'

Again everyone shrieked and wailed and cursed the foreigners.

'But our teachers aren't like that,' asserted Lanang. 'They love children and they love us. They would never do such a thing!'

'They are only pretending to be kind until they have taken us all in,' Re told him.

'But they teach our children before our very eyes. It would be impossible for them to kill a single child without our seeing.'

'Rongkau is a medicine man. He has seen it himself. He knows.'

'I shan't let my children run into the foreigners' house any more.'

'Neither shall I.'

'I won't have anything more to do with it.'

'I won't swallow a single pill.'

'Let's kill the foreigners when they come back.' The meeting was beginning to get hysterical.

'I doubt if they will come back,' Re said.

'But they've left their luggage here.'

'The Thai say that he has flown home with his wife.'

'I'm going back to the old way!' Lanang said. 'Tomorrow we'll put up a new altar and sacrifice to the spirits again.'

'So am I,' shouted several others.

'It's a pity our teacher isn't here; perhaps he could have answered our questions,' Lateng said thoughtfully.

'I'm staying on the new trail,' blurted out Nshu Seng, 'even if the teacher doesn't come back. Jesus is here. I'm not afraid.'

Everyone looked at him in dismay and a few laughed.

Nshu Seng got up, said 'Good-night' affably and went home. Tusang watched him go. What was it that made that little man so brave?

'You're mad!' somebody called after him.

Three days later, there was a great altar once more in the Chief's house. The Jesus posters had disappeared from a couple of other houses too. And then the cry rang through the village,

'The foreigner is back!'

Tusang and many others hurried across to the house on the hill of the spirits. It was already dark.

Thai were still carrying pieces of luggage into the house. The foreigner and his fair-haired wife were chatting to the few who had appeared to greet them.

'What's in that sack, Teacher?'

'Books, real Méo books, Tusang! Now we can begin teaching!' the teacher said happily. But no one showed any great enthusiasm.

'Aren't you glad that the first books have been printed at last?' the teacher asked, puzzled.

'Yes, but. . . .'

'Do you know that Lanang has left the new way?' blurted out Tusang.

'I have been told so but I can't believe it.' The teacher looked really upset.

'It's true Teacher.'

'Where is Nshu Seng?' the foreigner asked suddenly, looking round the group.

'At home. He's ill.'

'Ill?'

'Yes, Teacher, go and see him quickly. He said today: "If my illness doesn't go away, I am going back to the spirits." He needs you badly.'

'I'll go straight away.'

Tusang was lying on his platform but he couldn't sleep. What was he to think about all that had happened? It was too bad that that story of Rongkau's should have spoiled everything. Perhaps he had spread it round out of jealousy. The longed-for Méo books were there now, and they were beautiful, but who would want to learn to read?

'Don't be angry, Teacher,' said Lanang, 'but while you were away Rongkau said many wicked words against you. My brothers believed him. They were afraid. They came to me and implored me to build the altar again. I didn't want to but they compelled me. You didn't come back for such a long time we thought you would never return.'

'I still believe in Jesus. I will always remain your brother and your friend. Don't be afraid, Teacher, we have our Fuatai Jesus. Jesus is great. . . .'

Tusang had caught these words before he pushed the door open. He was curious to know what would happen next. The foreigner talked about Jesus, read out of the new books and prayed. Lanang had no desire, however, to burn his altar again.

'Never mind. Soon many brothers will know that our teacher is back. They will realize that you are a good man. Then we will all take the new way together. At the moment the people are afraid. They believe Rongkau. Jesus is sure to punish Rongkau and then they will all see that he is a liar.'

Nshu Seng appeared with his little boys.

'Are you better again, Nshu Seng?' Lanang was surprised to see him.

'Jesus has healed me,' he replied. 'The Teacher prayed with me and gave me an injection. Now the illness has almost gone. Praise and thanks be to God!'

'So now you won't put up your altar again?'

'No, certainly not! My family and I want to remain Jesus people.'

'Bear in mind that the Jesus way has become very steep, Nshu Seng.'

'Lanang, Jesus leads the way. He wore the crown of thorns. He bore the cross for me. Shouldn't I bear a cross too?'

The others were silent. The foreigner wiped his eyes, and he too said nothing.

'I must go home.' Nshu Seng changed the subject. 'Re wants to go hunting and he's waiting for me. Come and visit us, brothers.'

Tusang found this a suitable opportunity to disappear too.

For several weeks life went on in its usual pattern in the village. Tusang went to the teacher's from time to time. La and Nshu Seng were there almost every day to help with the translation, and they had both begun to read. Even Grandmother Seng Shua was taught by the teacher's wife every evening. Tusang had to laugh when he saw the old lady with her book in front of her nose or under her arm, but he couldn't help admiring her all the same. In spite of all the difficulties put in her path, she kept persistently on in the new way. There were only seven families now but they stood by one another staunchly, and allowed neither promises nor threats to deflect them from their course. Perhaps there really was something in this new religion.

Shuki was the most surprising—he had become a veritable demon. He went everywhere inciting people against this new way, and tried to make them drive the foreigners out of the village. He was unsuccessful, however, for many loved them in spite of everything, and those who did not were glad enough to accept their help.

Tusang had been away for three days on a hunting trip, and when he came back with a little roe buck, the old priest Shua Ying called to him from the distance.

'Tusang, I have some important news for you.'

Tusang stood in front of his neighbour, wondering.

'Your mother is ill,' whispered the old man.

'Ill?'

'Yes she has become insane. I wanted to prepare you for this terrible misfortune.'

'What? Insane? My mother has gone mad?'

'Wait, Tusang, don't run ahead; I'll tell you some more. It is no ordinary insanity, it is much worse.'

'What has happened? Out with it! Has someone bewitched her?'

'That's just it, Tusang, that's just it. She has been bewitched, and that by the two foreigners.'

'By the foreigners? How did it happen? Tell me!'

'I don't know really. In the last few months your mother has often been ill. From time to time she went to the foreigners for medicine—you know that yourself. In that way she has probably been bewitched.'

'I've certainly noticed that Mother has been calmer in these last few weeks than she used to be,' Tusang said thoughtfully. 'She's often said to me: "I am not going to have any more to do with my magic potions, they don't help at all." '

'Yes, and then yesterday she called the foreigners to her house. They sang and prayed, and later I saw how your mother and sister carried the altar out into the open and burnt it. The foreigners and a few Jesus people were there too.'

'What! Mother has burnt her altar? Impossible! I must go and see for myself.'

But it was true. The altar had disappeared, and there were no magic potions to be seen. A poster was hanging up instead, with a cross and these words written on it in both the Thai and Méo languages:

'Jesus says: I am the way, the truth and the life. No one comes to the Father but by me.'

Tusang was still standing looking at the poster when the door opened and his mother and sister appeared.

'Son, are you back already?'

'Yes, Mother. What's this poster here for?'

'Tusang! Your old mother has started out on the new trail. Don't be angry with me. I couldn't do anything else! Jesus has given me a new heart. I've done a lot of evil in my life, and I've failed often in my duty towards you, Tusang. Forgive me! But now Jesus will help me to walk in the new trail. Tusang, won't you set out wholeheartedly on this new way too?'

His mother looked at him appealingly.

'Mother, I have two hearts inside me. One wants to and the other does not want to—not yet. The way is too steep. I must have other brothers to join me first. I must also marry one day, then perhaps I'll join you on the new way.'

'Tusang,' said his sister, 'Mother and I are learning to read now. Look, I can read the first page fluently already!'

'Sister, surely you are not walking up the steep way too?'

'Yes, Tusang, I've already started. Jesus has come into my heart, and I'm so happy!'

'You're mad!' cried Tusang. He had to give vent to his tense feelings. 'You hardly know what it's about. Shuki and I have been writing the books for months on end, so we do know. We know it all. But you have been bewitched by the foreigners—bewitched and deranged!' He ran out of the shack.

Now this! Tusang had expected everything else, but not this. How could his mother do anything so insane? Deeply perturbed, he wandered about in the forest until he had calmed down. Then worn out, he began to make his way back to the village, saying under his breath,

'Perhaps they are right after all. Perhaps it's not they who are mad, but me. Perhaps the power of this Jesus is greater than I thought, and in the end He will reign over us Méo. Perhaps the new way is the right one. It's steep, but perhaps not too steep. At any rate some people seem to find joy in wanting to climb it.'

What was that? Familiar notes sounded in his ear. He realized he was standing right near the foreigners' shack, and strained to catch the words.

'I have decided
To follow Jesus . . .
No turning back, no turning back!

It was not only the foreigners singing. Resolute Méo voices, men, women, and children were joining in. Now they were continuing:

'Though no one joins me
Yet I will follow . . .
No turning back, no turning back!'

There was a half-rotten tree trunk lying in front of him. Tusang sat down on it and rested his head in his hands, wondering. The song had not yet come to an end. It seemed to go on ringing down the passage of the years ahead, when the little group must face persecution and sorrow, stumbling sometimes, triumphing sometimes. Joyfully this day they sang the song of their pilgrimage, as they set out along the new trail:

'The world behind me,
The cross before me . . .
No turning back, no turning back!'